Saving the world 1x1

Nature conservation, environmental protection & climate protection for beginners

How to recognize the problems of today's world and gradually improve them in small steps

Marieke Gesing

CONTENTS

What you can expect in this book

Our world is changing, the climate is changing. Species that have long existed on our planet are disappearing and resources are becoming scarce. People are slowly realizing that development is not always good. We are exploiting our earth, but we should be looking after it, because we only have this one. Slowly, however, a rethink is taking place and people are trying to undo past mistakes. Attempts are being made to reduce CO_2 emissions, conserve the earth's resources and pay more attention to nature. But once people have become accustomed to a certain standard of living, it is difficult to give it up again or change habits.

This book addresses the main problems facing our planet, discusses topics such as climate change, agricultural use, the energy transition and species extinction and provides advice and tips on how each individual can help to do something good for nature and the environment. It is up to everyone to make the world a better place.

Our world today

There are more people living on planet Earth today than ever before. In the last ten years, almost a billion people have been added, meaning that we will soon reach the eight billion mark. This naturally has consequences for nature and the environment.

In 2021, there will be 7.94 billion people on the planet. Above all, they need space to live and need to be fed. This in turn means an intensification of agriculture, which also requires space above all else. Space on earth and its resources are limited and as good as exhausted. In addition, all of these 7.79 billion people leave an ecological footprint, be it in the form of CO_2 emissions, the waste they produce or even the earth's resources they consume, such as gasoline. According to the organization 'Klima ohne Grenzen gemeinnützige GmbH', humanity's ecological footprint is currently so large that we would need 1.7 Earths for this way of life (klimaohnegrenzen.de, 2020).

The fact that there are now so many people on this earth and that capacities are gradually being exhausted has a number of consequences for nature. Pollution, global warming, acidification of the oceans, species extinction and much more are occurring. Of course, the whole process must be counteracted on a large scale.

But what can each and every one of us do in our everyday lives to make a small contribution to combating climate change, pollution and the like? In the following, individual aspects and consequences of overpopulation are addressed and small tips are given on how everyone can help to make the world a little bit better in their everyday lives.

The Earth ecosystem

In recent years in particular, and especially with the advance of science, it has become clear that all processes on Earth are interrelated, interdependent or even connected. The Earth's habitat is only the thin layer around the globe, from the deep sea trenches to the mountain peaks and the skies. These very different habitats are influenced by various factors and processes, but they are all connected in some way. The water cycle, plate tectonics, the composition of the atmosphere and the associated material cycles, winds and ocean currents show that planet Earth is a dynamic system whose main driving force is solar energy. If one component of this system changes, it makes the system fragile. This change, whether it is of anthropogenic or natural origin, can influence every other related process, with far-reaching and unpredictable consequences.

The climate is changing

But why is that? The climate has been changing ever since the earth has existed. There have been several ice ages in the Earth's past, but there have also been warm periods and the greenhouse effect occurred millions of years ago. According to a study by Kasting et al. (2003), this effect was responsible for the fact that at the beginning of the Earth's formation, although the sun was approx. 30 % less intense than today, the temperatures on Earth were still comparable to today's tempera-tures. This shows that the greenhouse effect can have an enormous influence on the Earth's climate. After the emergence of life on Earth, however, the climate always remained within ranges that also allow for such life.

The big difference to current global warming is that this process is not natural, but anthropogenic, and is progressing very quickly. In the history of the earth, we are talking about climate changes over millions of years. Today, significant changes in the climate can be observed within just a few years.

Burning fossil fuels emits greenhouse gases into the atmosphere. These gases, such as CO_2, methane and nitrous oxide, accumulate in the Earth's atmosphere. While the short-wave and high-energy radiation from the sun can pass through this layer of greenhouse gases more or less unhindered, the longer-wave heat rays that are reflected by the earth's surface are absorbed by the greenhouse gases and thus remain in the atmosphere, heating it up, similar to a greenhouse. However, this effect is nothing new for the earth, it actually occurs naturally and is extremely important for the warm climate on earth. The natural greenhouse effect is therefore necessary for life on earth, but the amplification of this effect through anthropogenic influences poses great dangers. The beginning of climate change today can be traced back to the time of industrialization. From this point onwards, global changes in the concentration of greenhouse gases in the atmosphere and therefore also changes in the climate can be recorded. The most effective greenhouse gas is methane, which mainly plays a role in livestock farming, as it is produced by cows during digestive processes. However, the much weaker greenhouse gas CO_2 plays the biggest role in the greenhouse effect due to the amount it emits, followed by methane and nitrous oxide.

GLOBAL WARMING

The greenhouse effect not only warms the Earth's atmosphere, but also the oceans through heat transfer, with enormous consequences. One of the biggest problems caused by this phenomenon is the slow melting of the polar ice caps. In contrast to the Antarctic, the Arctic is not a land mass covered in ice, but rather the Arctic Ocean, on which an area of pure ice several meters thick floats. If this enormous mass of ice melts, it causes several problems. The additional water masses will cause the world's oceans to rise by several meters. It must also be borne in mind that the polar ice is fresh water, which would dilute the current salt content of the sea when it melts. We can only assume what effects this will have on important ocean currents such as the Gulf Stream, which plays a large part in the mild climate in Europe. Furthermore, we know from core drillings deep into the ice masses that large quantities of methane gas are trapped in the ancient ice of the North Pole. A melting of the ice would mean the release of this methane gas, which in turn acts as a greenhouse gas and would intensify the greenhouse effect - a vicious circle.

Another problem caused by the rapid warming of the atmosphere and oceans is the shift in species ranges, both in the water and on land. Many animal and plant species are unable to adapt to the rapidly changing conditions. The species migrate to colder regions, if they can, or even die out regionally or globally. This is also the reason why, for example, diseases that until recently were only found in countries in warmer climate zones are appearing here. Carriers, mostly insects, now feel increasingly at home in the warmer Mediterranean regions and thus also reach Europe.

People tend to notice less about global warming itself; whether a year gets warmer on average is hardly noticeable to people. But what many people can probably confirm from their own experience is the increasingly extreme weather. Summers are getting hotter and drier, winters colder and wetter. In a few years' time, species that are quite common in our latitudes may soon no longer be found here. One example of this is spruce dieback. There are currently many dead spruce trees in the forest stands. This is because they are struggling to cope with the dry and hot conditions of recent summers and are also being weakened by parasites. In the future, it may be that our conventional cereals such as maize or wheat can no longer be grown in Germany because the conditions here are becoming too extreme. In the future, we may have to resort to species that can cope better with these more extreme conditions.

Polar bears in danger

Polar bears are at the top of the food chain and are one of the most dangerous animal species on e-arth. However, with increasing global warming and the associated melting of the polar ice caps, we must fear for the polar bears' habitat and thus for the species itself.

Polar bears spend most of their time on the ice hunting their main prey, seals. Polar bears find the best hunting conditions in winter. They only have to wait at the seals' breathing holes until they come up for air and can thus easily kill their prey. This is why the winter season in the Arctic is used by the big bears to eat "summer fat", as the summer season in the Arctic is leaner in terms of food.

However, researchers have noticed changes in the polar bears in their southernmost distribution area, Hudson Bay, in recent years. They are smaller and thinner and have fewer offspring. A correlation with the decline in ice has been established. Thinner layers of ice are more easily drifted by wind and ocean currents. For the polar bears, this means that they have to swim longer distances to get back onto other ice. Polar bears are very good swimmers, but in the ice-cold water this is very energy-consuming. The situation of the polar bears is not yet critical everywhere, but if we think of future summers in the Arctic without ice, this also raises fears for the future of the polar bears.

ACIDIFICATION OF THE OCEANS

It is not only the warming of the oceans that poses a problem for marine organisms. The CO_2 molecule has the ability to dissolve in water. According to a study by Jury et al. (2010), the world's oceans absorb around 25 % of the CO_2 present in the atmosphere. When dissolved in seawater, the CO_2 molecules enter into a chemical reaction with the water molecules, producing oxonium ions, which are responsible for the acidification of the world's oceans. If the oceans also become warmer, the capacity of the water to absorb CO_2 molecules from the atmosphere also increases - a vicious circle. This has far-reaching consequences for the inhabitants of the oceans. Species disappear, become extinct or are forced to retreat to colder regions. Coral reefs, which can only be surpassed by the biodiversity in tropical rainforests, no longer appear in their colorful splendor, but in brilliant white. What remains are the calcareous skeletons of the corals, which stretch for kilometers. Initially just a protective mechanism, the coral can survive in this state for another two weeks and eventually dies. Coral reefs also act as breakwaters and natural tsunami protection. However, a reef in this condition can no longer fulfill this function.

An additional problem is the disappearance of phytoplankton in the oceans. Phytoplankton are small diatoms that form the food source for zooplankton. Zooplankton is the main food source for numerous marine creatures such as blue whales, fin whales and baleen whales. Not only does the reduction of plankton endanger the existence of these sea creatures, but because they are algae, phytoplankton is also the most important oxygen producer on our planet, as the small algae carry out photosynthesis. They bind CO_2 and use it to produce between 50 and 80 % of the oxygen in the atmosphere. You can imagine what a loss these organisms would be in the fight against climate change.

But what can we do?

Of course, something must be done for the earth's climate, especially on a global scale, but it is also up to each individual. We can do so much ourselves in our everyday lives, especially to reduce CO_2 emissions. Here are a few small tips and tricks that everyone can take into account in their everyday lives:

• **Buy second-hand:** The production of clothes, furniture, cars etc. generates greenhouse gases that are pumped into the atmosphere. Reduce this by considering whether you would like to buy a second-hand product next time, for the sake of the environment.

• **Repair things instead of buying new ones:** Sometimes it's worth thinking about repairing things, which is often not only easy on the wallet, but also on the climate.

• **Use bicycles and public transport:** This is a point that we hear again and again, but one that should not be missed here either, as the proportion of car gas emissions plays a huge part in climate change. And with the current price of gasoline, it might really be worth taking the train or bus.

• **Buying organic products:** Everyone may have their own opinion about organic products. The fact is that these products are produced in a more climate-friendly way than products from conventional agriculture. So buy organic for the climate.

• **Eco-banks:** There are so-called eco-banks that take care when investing your money not to invest it in weapons development or climate-damaging companies. Instead, they invest in renewable energies and sustainable projects.

Development of agriculture

Agriculture is under enormous pressure these days. Farmers are the number one food producers of mankind. Billions of people have to be fed, which means a huge amount of food has to be produced. First and foremost, it has to be cheap. There are also a number of restrictions on what farmers can and cannot do, especially with regard to the climate. It is therefore difficult to do justice to all of these points, and many small regional farmers live on the breadline or even have to close their farms because it is no longer profitable.

For a long time, mankind was able to secure its food supply by expanding agricultural land at the expense of nature. Around half of the land in Germany is now used for agriculture. Space is limited and the area cannot be expanded indefinitely, so we now have to resort to the intensification of agriculture. Monocultures are grown using pesticides in order to achieve good harvests, and livestock is kept in confined spaces in order to keep production costs low. This has a number of consequences for nature and the environment, which are discussed below.

FRAGMENTATION OF THE LAND-SCAPE

The intensification of agriculture has led to drastic changes in our landscape. Over half of Germany's land is used for agriculture. This causes several problems. The landscape is fragmented and habitats are cut up. Mainly monocultures are cultivated, which offer no habitat for animals and other plants. There is one field next to the other. Less mobile animals are sometimes unable to overcome these barriers. A bee, for example, already finds it difficult to fly over a medium-sized field.

Animals such as the field hamster are disappearing because there is no more room for them. Habitat loss and habitat isolation are one of the biggest problems for biodiversity. However, in a fragmented landscape, factors such as the quality of the remaining habitats, above all the size of the habitats, but also the connectivity of the remaining habitats, can be decisive for the conservation of some species. Attempts are being made to remedy this by creating small islands where insects, birds and other animals can find food and a habitat. Some of you have probably already noticed the colorful flower strips at the edge of fields. Although these can provide temporary help for such species, flower strips are not a substitute for habitat and are not a permanent solution.

LIVESTOCK FARMING

Intensive livestock farming is also a problem for the climate. Not only animal husbandry under unethical conditions, but also the mass of slaughtered animals on earth poses a further threat to the climate. A study by the FAO Food and Agriculture Organization in 2006 examined the greenhouse gas emissions caused by livestock farming worldwide and found shocking figures: 18% of global greenhouse gas emissions are caused by livestock farming alone. Cattle in particular produce an enormous amount of the most effective greenhouse gas methane through digestive processes. First and foremost, however, is the fertilization of fields in connection with the provision of feed for all these farm animals. Another critical aspect of feed production is that agricultural land used for feed production cannot be used to produce food for humans. In many countries, including Germany, valuable ecosystems are being destroyed and even rainforests are being cleared to gain additional agricultural land for animal feed production. This is happening while there are people suffering from hunger in other parts of the world. A fact that needs to be questioned.

Not forgetting the use of agricultural vehicles and the production of fertilizers, which also contribute to greenhouse gas emissions. Reducing people's meat consumption would provide significant relief for the climate in many respects.

OVERFERTILIZATION

Liquid manure is a natural product and therefore does no harm if it is applied to the fields as fertilizer. This is not entirely true. Due to the increase in factory farming, liquid manure has become a waste product in abundance. Farmers don't know what to do with it and over-fertilize their fields. This has far-reaching consequences, as there is an excess of nutrients. Manure or fertilizers in general are characterized by their high nitrogen content. Nitrogen is one of the elementary building blocks of all living things on earth. However, plants and animals lack the ability to bind nitrogen from the air, where it makes up 78% of the air as an N_2 molecule. This task of binding nitrogen from the air is performed by microorganisms in the soil, which convert the nitrogen into the substance nitrate, which can be used by plants and humans.

This closes the so-called nitrogen cycle. When humans or animals eat plant-based food, they absorb the nitrate and then excrete it again. However, human intervention in the cycle disrupts it. This leads to an excess of nitrogen in the soil. This has a major impact on biodiversity, as it increasingly favours plants that have specialized in nutrient-rich soils. Species that rely on nutrient-poor soils are slowly disappearing. In addition, too much nitrogen also has an impact on the way plants grow. They grow much faster, but are less stable. This is why excess nutrients are also associated with forest dieback. The accelerated growth leads to crown thinning, which makes the trees more susceptible to drought and wind.

If the nitrogen in the soil is not completely absorbed by plants, soil acidification will increasingly occur. Species that predominantly occur in alkaline-rich locations are finding less and less habitat. Nitrogen is also playing an increasingly important role in water quality, both in drinking water and in surrounding bodies of water. An excessively high nitrogen content in water is a sign of poor water quality.

In addition, the excessive spreading of liquid manure also harbors another danger: Due to the heavy antibiotic treatment in factory farming, multi-resistant germs are repeatedly created in the stables, which then do not remain in the stables but are spread on the fields with the liquid manure.

PESTICIDE USE

With the intensification of agriculture and the expansion of agricultural land, more and more pesticides are being used worldwide. This poses a major threat to biodiversity. It is not the quantity that plays a role, as is often assumed, but the intensity of the substances used. For this reason, legal regulations on the quantity of a particular substance to be used are usually pointless. The use of broad-spectrum insecticides and herbicides has changed drastically since agricultural development. When used, they not only harm the target organisms, but also numerous other species groups, which slowly but surely leads to the impoverishment of agricultural fauna and flora.

Through the food chain, not only insects are usually affected, but also birds and mammals. In addition, there is always the risk that these substances seep into the soil and reach the groundwater.

But what can we do?

The consumer determines the offer. This applies more to this point than to any other described in this book. We determine the development of agriculture through our purchasing behavior. This is a point where each individual has a particularly large influence. Here are a few tips and hints on how to protect nature:

• **Buy regional products:** You can help the climate enormously by using regional products. Transporting food from one place to another by ship, plane or truck is a significant contributor to climate change and greenhouse gas emissions.

• **Buy seasonally: in other words,** if you buy raspberries in winter or pumpkins in spring, you can be sure that they most likely do not come from Germany. There are certain growing seasons for fruit and vegetables here in Germany, stick to these seasons and you can be sure that the produce you are buying has been produced in Germany and has not been transported over long distances.

• **Eat less meat:** The meat industry is a major contributor to climate change and the terrible conditions in which animals are kept make you question humanity. Perhaps think about reducing your meat consumption a little, and if it is to be meat, look for regional products with good animal husbandry.

• **Against food waste:** try not to throw food away. The production of this food has already had a negative impact on the climate. So many tons of food are simply thrown away every year, a fact that is hardly ethically justifiable when many people in other regions of the world are suffering from hunger. There are now also many offers, e.g. to buy bread from the day before or food with an expired best-before date, so take up these offers more often for the sake of the climate.

Climate & Energy

Humans are consuming the earth's resources faster than the earth can produce them, mainly to produce energy - the basis of modern society. Nowadays, we need energy for most everyday things. Worldwide, 13,000 million tons of crude oil are used to produce energy every year. In comparison, the average German citizen consumes around 1.25 tons of oil per year in the form of energy. This figure has risen steadily since industrialization. Most of this energy is obtained by burning fossil fuels such as gas, coal or oil. This has two major disadvantages: Burning them produces greenhouse gases that harm the climate, and fossil fuels are finite. Against this background, it is particularly tragic that only a third of the energy produced can later be used as final energy. One third is lost during energy conversion and transportation, etc. The other third are losses caused by the consumer.

These losses do not occur with electricity generated directly from renewable energies such as hydropower, wind power or photovoltaics. Today, around 23% of energy is generated from renewable sources, and the trend is rising. The world is already changing and this has already been reflected in politics. In the next few years, for example, the lignite industry and nuclear power are to be phased out and the focus will increasingly be on wind and solar power.

UNLIMITED ENERGY

Renewable energy sources are available to people indefinitely; the only limitation is when the weather does not cooperate, the sun does not shine or the wind does not blow. From a physical point of view, the term renewable energy is also not entirely correct, as energy is neither destroyed nor created. Energy is always there and can merely be converted into other forms.

Bioenergy

Bioenergy accounts for the largest share of energy produced from renewable sources in Germany. Here, heat, electricity and fuel are produced from solid, liquid or gaseous components. This method is very versatile as it does not depend on a single source product. Both plant and animal waste products can be used, as well as other renewable raw materials. In Germany, the production of bioenergy is most important for heating, but also for the production of fuel.

Wind power

Wind power also plays a key role in the production of clean energy. After bioenergy, wind energy represents the second largest share of energy production from renewable sources. Wind energy is converted into electricity using wind turbines based on the windmill principle. These turbines can be located both on land and at sea. However, the construction of these so-called offshore plants is much more challenging than the installation of conventional wind turbines on land. These turbines are usually located 30-40 km from the coast in water depths of up to 40 meters. It is easy to imagine that the connection to the electricity grid and the stable anchoring of the turbines at such water depths represent an enormous challenge.

Photovoltaics

The generation of electricity from solar energy also plays a key role in Germany. This technology is the most cost-effective of all technologies that produce electricity from renewable energy sources. Sunlight is converted directly into electricity in the solar cells. Hardly any maintenance is required for these systems, which is why this technology is also very well suited for use in countries with a poorly developed supply grid.

Hydropower

Hydropower is used less in Germany, but is very valuable in other parts of the world. It has great potential for generating electricity, but is dependent on the amount of precipitation and geographical conditions. In a waterworks, the kinetic energy of the water is used to generate electricity. The water's flow speed sets a turbine in motion, which in turn drives a generator to produce electricity.

Conclusion on renewable energies
The production of electricity from renewable energies also requires interventions in ecosystems. In some cases, large plants are installed that have an impact on animals and plants. For example, wind turbines often cause bird strikes and bats also have problems in the vicinity of the turbines, as their sonar is affected or even destroyed by the rotating rotor blades. The use of hydropower also leads to changes in ecosystems. Water is dammed up in places where there was previously no water, other places are drained where there has always been water. In some countries, there are also ethical conflicts between generating electricity and providing water for people who depend on it. Furthermore, damming changes natural tidal processes, which are often very important for the fertility of the soil. There are also risks

associated with the installation of solar systems, as they require space. This also changes the landscape.

But what are our alternatives? After all, people need energy to live, and in no small measure. Nobody is prepared to give up the standard of living that has been established over decades, which is why we have to look for solutions to the energy problem. Compared to the generation of energy from lignite or nuclear power, the impact of energy generation from renewable sources can probably be classified as minor.

But what can we do?

We can make ourselves aware that electricity is a valuable commodity and that the climate suffers for its production. If we become a little more aware of this, saving electricity may not be so difficult. There are lots of simple tricks that everyone can follow in their everyday lives.

- **Support clean energy (wind, solar and water):** There are already electricity providers that specialize in clean energy. Perhaps a switch would be an option for you?

• **Solar panels: You can** also actively do something by considering installing a solar system on your roof. If you don't want to make too big an investment, you can buy individual solar panels at a reasonable price and set them up in the garden or on the balcony, for example. This is easy on the wallet and the climate.

• **Appliances with low energy consumption:** All household appliances such as dishwashers, tumble dryers and fridges have information on how much electricity they consume. Perhaps you will pay less attention to the design and more to the energy consumption the next time you buy an appliance.

• **Use LED lamps:** Replacing normal light bulbs with LED bulbs is a very simple matter. These use only 20 % of the electricity of conventional light bulbs.

• **Save energy in general:** In general, it is important not to waste energy. Simply saving energy by switching off the lights when you are not in the room or switching off the TV or laptop when you are not using them can work wonders.

• Eco function for household appliances:
Many appliances, such as dishwashers or washing machines, already have integrated eco functions. It probably takes a little longer to use these, but it does something for the environment.

Species decline - the sixth major species extinction

There have already been five major species extinctions in the history of the earth. One of these, for example, was triggered by the meteorite impact millions of years ago, which led to the extinction of the dinosaurs and so many other species. Today, humans are witnessing and causing the sixth great mass extinction on Earth. The extinction of species is generally a natural process of selection that is constantly taking place on Earth. However, biodiversity is now being lost at a dramatic and unnatural rate.

Historically, the biggest cause of species extinction in human history has been hunting. In the past, many animal species were hunted to extinction for their fur or meat, as people at the time did not know any better and it was a matter of survival. However, this changed as time went on. The main cause of species extinction today is the destruction and fragmentation of habitats, as well as fishing. The spread of invasive species and climate change (e.g. coral reefs) also have an impact.

There are many reasons why we should not simply stand by and watch this loss of species. Apart from the fact that we have an ethical obligation to take care of our ecosystems, many ecosystems also provide something for humans. Without them, life as we know it is no longer possible on Earth.

Plants are essential for humans and animals both as a food source and as animal feed. By carrying out photosynthesis, they are the equivalent of humans and animals, as they generate oxygen from CO_2, while humans and animals need oxygen to live and exhale CO_2 as a waste product. Plants therefore also play an important role in the material cycle. In addition, we would no longer be able to make use of the effects of medicinal plants if they were to fall victim to species loss. **Forests play** a very important role in that they regulate the climate, act as a CO_2 sink and bind the CO_2 that we produce. Forests are also essential for filtering water and protecting against erosion. Wood as a building material is also of great importance to people. **Farm animals** are important in that they help to feed humanity. They provide meat, milk, eggs, wool and other raw materials. Farm animals also play a role in many countries as their labor is used. **Insects are the** number one pollinators on earth. They pollinate three quarters of all flowering plants. Without them, fruit trees and many other plant species would be a thing of the past. They also play a very important role in the food chain, providing staple food for numerous other animal species. They also have a function in the decomposition of waste and waste products. **Microorganisms** such as bacteria and protozoa are particularly important for decomposition processes. They return minerals to the material cycles and thus to nature. Without them, life on earth in its present form would not be possible.

We need all these species groups, the earth needs them. If, as predicted, 30-50% of species do indeed become extinct in the near future, we will have to ask ourselves whether biological processes and ecosystems are still as efficient as they are today or whether they might even disappear completely. As already described, planet Earth is a large ecosystem. If parts of this system come to a standstill, will the Earth really still function as a whole? If so many species disappear, this will have unforeseeable consequences for every aspect of our lives.

THE ROLE OF INVASIVE SPECIES

Invasive species are species that do not occur naturally in a certain region but have nevertheless spread there. These have usually been introduced to these regions by humans, both intentionally and unintentionally. Reasons for the introduction of new species into areas of the world where they do not occur naturally include pleasure, but also the provision of food. For example, crops are cultivated in regions that are not the natural habitat of these species. In addition, humans have introduced hunting game to some parts of the world in order to introduce a new food source, often with unexpected consequences. The unintentional introduction of species mainly occurs on transport routes, whether through trade or by vacation travelers.

The introduction of non-native species often has unforeseen effects on ecosystems. As the species are often generalists that can cope well under a wide range of living conditions, they become established in the new regions. Very often, they then compete with the native species for habitat and resources such as food or shelter. In most cases, the native species lose out and are slowly pushed out of their habitat. However, not only larger animals are affected, but also microorganisms and fungi, as the next example shows.

The world's amphibian species are currently threatened by a new danger. A fungus is currently spreading that occurs naturally in Africa on so-called clawed frogs, but is deadly for other amphibian species. In the 1960s in particular, these frogs were deliberately spread all over the world, with the result that many amphibian species have since fallen victim to the fungus. Even today, efforts are still being made to combat the fungus.

Another interesting example can be found in New Zealand. The island split off from other land masses early on in the Earth's history, giving a very special fauna the opportunity to develop. As there were no large predators on the island, the group of flightless birds developed. Kiwi, kakapo and co. were able to develop undisturbed until predators such as rats or the possum, native to North America, were brought to New Zealand with the settlers. As you can imagine, the birds that cannot fly are easy prey and are now threatened with extinction.

INSECT MORTALITY - WHEN THE LITTLE ONES DISAPPEAR

A long-term study by Hallmann et al. (2017) caused quite a stir a few years ago. The study examined 60 locations over 27 years for the insects (biomass) found there. The results were shocking. Within the 27 years, the biomass of insects fell by

75 %. But what is the reason for this and can we even stop this trend?

There are various causes of insect mortality, but they all have one thing in common: they are man-made. One of the most decisive reasons is the change in the landscape. A small, parceled-out and species-rich cultural landscape with fallow land, orchards and numerous hedgerow structures has become a monotonous and structurally poor agricultural desert that offers no habitat for wild animals and plants. The intensification of agriculture has added to the problems of pesticide use and over-fertilization. With recurring crop rotations and monocultures, farmers are breeding resistant pests and have to resort to increasingly effective pesticides. In addition, the combination of different pesticides on the insect fauna has hardly been studied.

The use of pesticides does not stop at forests either, as forestry is the second most important land use. To combat the gypsy moth and other insects, the forests are also liberally sprayed to protect the already vulnerable monocultures and contain the spread of the pests. There is an additional problem for the numerous nocturnal insects: light pollution. Attracted by the artificial light, many die of exhaustion and are disoriented. Three percent of our land area is taken up by private gardens. These would be such important oases of biodiversity in today's highly impoverished cultural landscape, but the use of pesticides and the sterile design of the gardens mean that they only provide a habitat for a few insect species.

Not all honey bees are the same
The biggest difference for humans is that wild bees do not produce honey, but they are at least as important as honey bees. In contrast to honey bees, wild bees do not live in colonies, but are solitary, i.e. they are loners. They therefore take care of the rearing of their offspring on their own. For example, they dig tunnels in the ground or in wood, nest in flower stems or use snail shells to lay their eggs. There is great diversity among wild bees, but they need nesting sites and suitable material to reproduce successfully. There are around 550 species of wild bee in Germany, many of which are threatened with extinction due to habitat loss and agriculture. Over half are on the Red

List. In contrast, however, 80% of wild plants and over 150 crops depend on pollination by wild bees. It is very interesting to note that the more often a flower is visited by different wild bees, the larger the fruit. This means that a third of the crop yield is directly related to the number of pollinations and therefore also the number of wild bees in general.

If you want to do something specifically for wild bees, here are a few tips on what wild bees particularly like:

- **Kitchen herbs on the balcony or in the garden:** Wild bees love culinary herbs such as borage, thyme, sage, marjoram or rosemary. Let the herbs bloom and make them available to the wild bees.
- **Spring flowers:** Wild bees are also dependent on early blooming flowers. They particularly like crocuses, snowdrops and hyacinths.
- **Trees and shrubs:** Wild bees love fruit trees. With numerous blossoms, they can provide many wild bees with food. So plant fruit trees and berry bushes such as apple trees, pears, cherries, currant or gooseberry bushes for the bees.

• **Wildflower meadow:** You can also help with a beautiful wildflower meadow, whether in flower pots or small plots in the garden, the wild bees will thank you. A little tip: Wildflowers grow particularly well in poor soil. Store-bought potting soil is often too rich in nutrients, but by adding sand or gravel you can easily thin it out.

• **Leave faded shrubs standing:** Do not cut off the faded stems and shrubs in the fall, as they provide wild bees with shelter for the winter.

Help for butterflies

Butterflies don't have it easy these days either. Just like wild bees, butterflies are also being pushed back by habitat loss and the use of pesticides. There are around 3,500 species of butterflies and moths in Germany. Of these, 190 belong to the colorful and magnificent butterflies that we immediately associate with the term butterfly. The majority, however, are rather inconspicuous moths. Among the butterflies there are generalists and the often more endangered specialists. They are, for example, tied to a specific food plant or very specific environmental conditions. One such example is the blue butterfly, which, as its name suggests, lays its caterpillars in the meadow knob of the same name.

The larvae are dependent on the plant not being mown and the meadow knob remaining standing until they have completed their development. This is often somewhat difficult, as the meadow knob is often found in pastures or hay meadows. The evening primrose hawk moth has also specialized in a particular food plant, the evening primrose. These species are therefore particularly endangered as they are heavily dependent on specific plant species. However, all butterflies have one thing in common: the development from egg, to caterpillar, to pupa and finally to moth. Many plants depend on butterflies as pollinators. With their long proboscis, they can reach deep into plant calyxes to drink the nectar.

If you want to support butterflies, you will find a few tips below on what butterflies like. It differs only slightly from what you can do for wild bees:

• **Herb garden:** Butterflies also love herbs that bloom. Butterflies' favorite herbs include thyme, lavender, mint and lemon balm.

• **Wildflower meadow on poor soils:** By sowing a wildflower meadow, you are doing something for both wild bees and butterflies at the same time.

• **Plants for the caterpillars:** Even in the caterpillar stage, moths need to eat. Caterpillars particularly prefer shrubs such as blackberries or raspberries, but fennel, violets, hawthorn and vetches are also on their menu.

• **Flower lawns:** Allow the low-growing flowers that naturally occur in your lawn to thrive. Tip: If you don't want to leave the entire lawn standing, leave small islands of lawn where not only butterflies feel at home.

• **Overwintering quarters:** Butterflies also need somewhere to spend the winter. Stone and brushwood piles, dense ivy or wild vines are suitable for this.

• **Potting soil without peat: Peat** extraction destroys bogs, an important habitat for butterflies and other species. You should therefore avoid potting soil that contains peat.

THE DECLINE IN BIRDS

The number of bird species occurring in Germany and their numbers have fallen drastically. This particularly affects the birds of the agricultural landscape. Almost three quarters of the bird species native to Germany are now on the Red List. There has been a particularly alarming decline in the populations of lapwing, partridge, black-tailed godwit and whinchat (85-60 % decline). There are several reasons for the decline in bird populations, but the most decisive factor is the lack or loss of suitable habitats. The simultaneous extinction of insects has also led to a lack of food supply. Insect mortality and the decline in bird numbers are therefore directly linked. Another reason is the excessive use of pesticides and fertilizers in agriculture. These figures once again show the negative impact of monocultures and chemicals on biodiversity.

THE CURRENT PROBLEM OF THE FIELD HAMSTER

The field hamster, which is native to Germany, is also slowly but surely disappearing from the scene. It is already classified as critically endangered on the Red List. The nocturnal animal belongs to the native mammal fauna and is found in Central to Eastern Europe and parts of Asia. A few years ago, the field hamster was still widespread throughout Germany and was considered a plague, as it lived in the local grain fields and helped itself to the buffet in abundance. Today, the field hamster is only found in a few areas with equally small populations. The field hamster has high demands on its habitat. For example, the soil must contain sufficient loam and loess. On the one hand, this increases the yield of the crops growing there and, on the other, the burrows can be dug more easily in this soil composition. The field hamster spends most of the day in its burrow and only comes out at night to forage for food.

There are various reasons why the European hamster is so threatened. One important factor is the structural change in the landscape. Initially, the field hamster benefited from the expansion of agriculture, but today's monocultures and fast, highly efficient harvesting machines are also too much for the field hamster and are partly responsible for the sharp decline in numbers. In addition, one-sided cultivation, a lack of variety in crop rotation and the use of pesticides and fertilizers are further affecting the hamster. Another problem for the field hamster is the increasing sealing of areas during road construction or the construction of new industrial areas. As a result, potential habitat for the field hamster is completely lost. The fragmentation of the landscape, also due to roads or highways, makes it almost impossible for individuals to migrate in and out of the individual populations. There is no genetic exchange, the gene pool is impoverished and this again has a negative impact on the reproduction rates of the hamsters. Another deadly trap is traffic. The European hamster is one of the most frequent victims. This is due to its defensive behavior towards predators.

If a supposed enemy (in this case the car) approaches quickly, the little hamster stands up on its hind legs, makes itself big and starts hissing and jumping at the enemy, true to the motto "attack is the best defense". Unfortunately, this is less likely to help with an approaching car. Predation also plays a role today. The European hamster has a number of natural enemies, such as birds of prey, the fox and the badger. In a healthy population density, the relationship between predators and prey is in harmony and subject to cyclical fluctuations. In a population that is under attack and whose reproduction numbers are not correct, the loss of each animal is tragic and brings the population a little closer to extinction.

There are now numerous projects that have set themselves the task of halting the decline in the numbers of the European hamster and enabling the hamster to coexist with today's agriculture. One project called 'Feldhamsterland', for example, works very closely with local farmers who volunteer to help protect the European hamster. For example, staff are available to provide advice and suggest measures on how best to help the European hamster in a particular region. But that's not all: there are also numerous projects in which hamsters are bred and reintroduced into the wild, and the development of the reintroduced populations is documented in order to learn more details about the species.

But what can we do for biodiversity?
Many of the endangered animals can also be found in our gardens. A near-natural garden design can increase biodiversity enormously.

• **Flower mixtures for bees, bumblebees and others:** Do you have a small corner free in your garden and don't know what to do with it? Why not think about sowing a mini flowering meadow for insects? Next summer you will see that many insects are happy to take up the offer.

• **Deadwood in the garden:** Perhaps leave the cut tree lying around or get a nice root and decorate your garden with it. This not only looks beautiful, but also provides a habitat for numerous insects.

• **Insect hotel:** You can buy so-called insect hotels, but there are also great instructions for building your own. These offer numerous insects a great place to spend the winter.

• **Robot lawn mowers:** These robots are particularly dangerous for hedgehogs. Hedgehogs are repeatedly injured by them. What's more, a short-cut lawn offers no habitat. So maybe mow a little less, then you can be sure that you will have more animals of all kinds in your garden.

• **Nature-oriented design: In** general, the more nature-oriented you design your garden, the more animals will find a habitat there. If your garden is tidy and sterile, few animals will feel at home there.

Pollution - what to do with our waste?

In Europe, each person produces around 500 kg of waste every year. However, only 40% of this is recycled, even though it is largely made up of recyclable materials such as plastic, paper and glass. A further 40% is sent to landfill and the rest of the waste produced is incinerated. This is particularly harmful to the environment, as waste incineration produces greenhouse gases such as CO_2, which further fuel climate change. In addition, the low percentage of recycling means that the earth's already scarce resources are being exploited.

Another problem is that too many waste particles end up in the environment and landfills, waste incineration plants or recycling stations are bypassed. This waste in the environment poses a major problem, especially for wildlife, but also for entire ecosystems. It is clear that less waste needs to be produced in general and the percentage of recycling needs to be increased.

PLASTIC WASTE

It is estimated that 150 million tons of plastic waste are floating in the oceans, and nine million tons are added every year. No one knows whether this figure is realistic or not, as the extent of waste pollution is immense and difficult to estimate. The ocean currents cause the plastic waste to collect in so-called garbage patches. There are currently five huge plastic islands in the sea. The best-known garbage patch is the "Great Pacific Garbage Patch" (GPGP), which is located in the North Pacific current between Hawaii and California. At 1.6 million m^2 , this garbage patch is three times the size of France and has an estimated weight of 100 million tons. It should not be forgotten that this garbage vortex consists exclusively of garbage.

Most types of plastic are made from crude oil or gas and are extremely durable. Plastic parts remain in nature for several hundred years before they slowly begin to decompose. Against this backdrop, the production of single-use plastics seems unethical and disproportionate, as these items have already fulfilled their purpose after a single use and end up as waste in nature, landfills and incinerators.

It is estimated that more than 800 marine animal species are affected by the plastic problem. They mistake plastic particles for food, for example, and eat them. The stomach is full, but the animals cannot digest the plastic and eventually starve to death with a full stomach. Fibrous plastic particles such as fishing nets and much more are also a deadly trap. Animals become entangled in these and die as they are unable to free themselves on their own. There are also problems with plastic waste that are not immediately visible. Depending on the type of plastic, plasticizers are added which gradually dissolve from the plastic. Plastic particles also have the ability to absorb environmental toxins. These then collect on the surface and poison many marine animals that ingest these particles voluntarily or involuntarily.

Only 6% of plastic waste floats on the surface of the water, which makes it difficult to estimate the extent of marine litter pollution. The rest of the waste sinks to the seabed with unpredictable long-term consequences. Floating in the water, the plastic becomes brittle and breaks down into smaller and smaller particles. This is by no means a positive degradation process.

THE PROBLEM OF MICROPLASTICS

Microplastics are solid synthetic plastic particles that are smaller than 5 mm. Microplastics can be created by the decomposition of larger plastic parts (secondary microplastics). On the other hand, microplastics are also produced directly in this size for industrial purposes (primary microplastics). Definitions and names for plastics of different sizes can be found below:

• Megaplastics: plastic parts with a size of over 100 mm

- Macroplastics: plastic parts with a size of more than 25 mm
- Mesoplasty: plastic parts with a size of between 5 and 25 mm
- Microplastics: plastic parts with a size between 0.0001 and 5 mm
- Primary microplastics: pellets, textile fibers, tire abrasion, microbeads in cosmetics
- Secondary microplastics are created by the decomposition of larger plastic parts
- Nanoplastics: plastic parts with a size of less than 0.0001 mm
- Primary nanoplastics: particles in electronics, biomedical products or paints/lacquers
- Secondary nanoplastics are created by the decomposition of larger plastic parts

It's not just microplastics that are found in the oceans, rivers and lakes by the millions. Microplastics can now be found everywhere, even in places where you wouldn't really expect them. It has already reached the most remote regions of our planet, such as the Arctic, Antarctic and Alpine lakes. Microplastics are spread on fields with manure, they can be found in fruit and vegetables, in water and even in beer. Last but not least, microplastics have even been detected in the human body. There have only been a few studies on the effects of plastic in our bodies so far. However, we can imagine that, just like in the oceans, it also has negative effects on our bodies.

THE OCEAN CLEANUP

The Ocean Cleanup is a great project launched by a young and committed Dutchman called Boyan Slat. He set himself the goal of combating the pollution of the oceans with plastic waste and has therefore developed a collection system that autonomously collects plastic from the oceans. Various smaller prototypes have already been successfully tested and are in use. The next step is to develop a full-scale system.

The system consists of a 600 m long floating body made of polyethylene pipes, to which a kind of skirt is attached to collect plastic parts from up to 3 m deep water. The floating body has a U-shape and can therefore collect and hold plastic pieces like in a bay. In addition to cleaning up the oceans, The Ocean Cleanup also deals with the removal and recycling of the collected plastic waste. This means that 100% of the plastic waste from the oceans is recycled.

But what can we do?

• **Avoid plastic waste:** When shopping, try to choose products without plastic packaging. The use of plastic bags should also be avoided. Perhaps you will remember to bring your own containers the next time you visit the sausage or cheese counter to avoid the store's plastic packaging. In some larger cities, there are even stores that do not use plastic packaging at all, so you can also use your own lunch boxes and containers. Take advantage of this offer.

• **Avoid wrapping paper:** This is coated paper, which cannot be recycled like normal paper. Perhaps you should simply use a gift bag for your next present or decorate normal paper yourself.

• **Cosmetics with microplastics:** Cosmetics are something you really don't expect to find microplastics in. But microplastics are used in scrubs in particular for the rough effect. Look out for microplastic-free products when buying cosmetics and toiletries.

• **Litter in the environment:** Litter that has already ended up in the environment is a major problem. Perhaps you happen to have a bag with you and can collect the garbage and dispose of it in the garbage can at home. Nature will thank you for it.

• **Waste separation: Make sure you** separate your waste correctly, if the waste in the waste stations cannot be sorted, it will be sent to landfill or incineration and cannot be recycled.

• **The Ocean Cleanup:** Perhaps you are looking for a project that you can support in the future. The Ocean Cleanup is a good example of young, committed people who care about the future of the planet.

Future strategies and projects

THE CLIMATE

One of the biggest threats to humanity and life as we know it is climate change. Something needs to be done, and quickly. Politicians also see this, which is why the Paris Agreement was launched in 2015. At the 21st Climate Change Conference in Paris, 55 countries signed an agreement that set uniform climate targets. Today, all countries in the world, with the exception of the USA, are members. The main objective of the agreement is to limit global warming caused by human activity to well below 2°C. The countries also undertake to define voluntary measures and contributions to limit global warming and to monitor these. The other countries will review these and make any necessary adjustments. It remains to be seen what results this agreement will produce over the next few years. The question is whether voluntary commitments and voluntary contributions to climate change are the right way to save our planet given the current situation.

How does the magical 2°C limit come about? You only have to look at what would happen if the earth warmed by the aforementioned 2°C: according to predictions and estimates, sea levels would rise, which would spell the end for many island states, especially smaller ones. In addition, an estimated ten million people in coastal regions would be increasingly affected by flooding. In the Mediterranean region and southern Africa, on the other hand, there would be a 20-30% reduction in available water.

But is the goal of staying below 2 °C realistic? The earth is already 1.1 °C warmer today. Due to the inertia of the climate, the temperature would initially continue to rise even if greenhouse gas emissions were stopped immediately. The IPCC prepared a special report to discuss what is needed to meet the agreed targets. For example, greenhouse gas emissions must be reduced by 45% by 2030, and by 2050 greenhouse gas emissions must be at net zero, i.e. no more greenhouse gases must be emitted than can be neutralized by the ecosystems.

The consequences of climate change usually affect those who have the least stake in it. Countries around the world have different levels of greenhouse gas emissions and are working differently hard to reduce them. Unfortunately, however, climate change is global and also affects those who have hardly any share in greenhouse gas emissions. Bangladesh, for example, has a CO_2 value of a quarter of a ton per capita per year. Unfortunately, the country's inhabitants are feeling the effects of climate change particularly hard in the form of rising sea levels, with frequent flooding due to the country's low lying location. The main perpetrators of today's climate change are to be found in the old industrialized countries. The largest CO_2 producer today is China. Only if everyone works together and pulls in the same direction will we come a step closer to the goal of staying below 2 °C.

Agriculture is under particularly great pressure. By 2050, farmers will probably have to feed ten billion people on earth and also provide raw materials for clean bioenergy, preferably without resorting to pesticides and fertilizers. But this is a dead end. In the past, the development of fertilizers and pesticides has contributed enormously to increasing agricultural productivity. However, as the environmentally damaging effects of these products are now well known, their use cannot be increased any further and must in fact be reduced. In addition, space is also exhausted, which means that agricultural land can no longer be expanded - the second factor that increased productivity in the past. People therefore have to think of something completely new in order to achieve the next stage in increasing agricultural productivity. There are two different strategies that can be pursued. There is "green genetic engineering" versus the optimization of peasant agriculture. But what does that mean?

Genetic engineering has a very bad reputation, but genetically modified plants can actually bring enormous benefits. A desired gene (DNA segment) from one organism is introduced into another organism, such as crops, using a vector. For example, a gene from the bacterium *Bacillus thuringiensis* was transferred into cotton so that the plants can now produce a substance that is toxic to insects. The insects avoid these plants without the need to continue using pesticides. The vision is to create crops that can better cope with increasing drought and drought stress, as well as better utilize the nitrogen in the soil. Both would result in an enormous increase in productivity. On the other hand, there is organic farming. The aim here is to use the functional principles of ecosystems to increase productivity. The focus is on healthy soil, healthy plants, healthy animals and healthy people. But is that enough? Studies show that this would be enough to feed the world's population, but meat consumption per capita would have to be halved. Currently, each person eats an average of 37 kg of meat per year, with every German eating as much as 60 kg.

ENERGY

There are two strategies being pursued to ensure that affordable energy will continue to be available for so many people on earth in the future: One is to make better and more efficient use of energy without major losses, and the other is to replace fossil fuels with renewable energy. All energy produced, whether from fossil fuels or renewable energies, has consequences and pollutes the environment. For this reason, the efficiency strategy must be pursued further in the future. The conversion of various forms of energy and their transportation generate enormous losses that must be reduced at all costs. One weak point for such energy losses is the generation of electricity in thermal power plants. Thermal power plants have an efficiency of only 39%, while more modern plants achieve 53%. This means that not even half of the energy generated in such power plants is used. The problem is the heat loss during the conversion of the energy, the so-called waste heat. The aim must be to be able to use this in the future, and that is exactly what is planned. A heat transport network must be created for this purpose and large, centralized power plants must be replaced by smaller, more efficient power plants. This would allow nearby households to use the plant's waste heat for heating in the form of local or district heating.

Another point are so-called combined heat and power plants. Here, the electricity is no longer purchased exclusively from the energy supplier, but electricity can be generated by installing a heater with a special motor. With such small private systems, the costs for the heat distribution infrastructure are eliminated. This is also particularly worthwhile for the climate, as long transportation routes and the associated energy losses are kept to a minimum.

Care should also be taken to build energy-efficient homes. In Germany, 150 kWh/m^2 is used for heating in a normal home. In so-called passive houses, this value can be reduced to just 15 kWh/m^2 . This is achieved primarily through a very well insulated and tight building envelope. In addition, the windows are triple-glazed. A crucial point is the ventilation system with heat recovery, where it is sufficient to heat the air supplied. During the warm season, heat recovery from the sun and the electrical appliances used is usually sufficient.

ECOSYSTEMS

Functioning ecosystems on Earth are the source of life and also the source of our prosperity. The majority of the earth's ecosystems have already been destroyed, making it all the more important that the remaining ecosystems remain functional. These must withstand the increasing pressure of human use. An important tool here is the designation of new protected areas. There must be more areas on earth where the protection of species and habitats takes precedence over economic interests. It is particularly important to protect the remaining functioning large habitats, such as the Amazon region. But global hotspots of species must also be given extra protection. The size of the areas plays a subordinate role here. However, corridors between the protected areas are important in order to ensure connectivity. This allows individuals to migrate in and out, which is particularly important for the genetic diversity of species.

It's not too late

It's not too late to save our planet and too early to give up, but the traffic light is dark orange. Something needs to happen globally and many countries need to get involved to make a difference. Something has to happen and giving up is not an option. After all, it's about our planet and its beautiful nature, which we are exploiting and slowly destroying. There needs to be a rethink and everyone needs to understand what is at stake here. Sooner or later, the world will recover from what we have done to it. But no one knows whether humanity will still be part of this world.

It's not too late, it's in our hands. Together we can achieve so much and together we can also overcome this crisis. If we care about the future of our children and their children, we have to start acting now. Every single one of us is needed. There are small things we can do for our planet, but we have to be willing and open to them. Help for our planet, because we only have this one.

www.ingramcontent.com/pod-product-compliance
Lightning Source LLC
Chambersburg PA
CBHW031501130726
47989CB00003B/1494